EVER
OF 1983

NEWS FOR EVERY DAY OF THE YEAR

Sean Connery and Saskia Cohen-Tanugi on a promotional tour for the James Bond film *Never Say Never Again*, 23 November 1983.

By Hugh Morrison

MONTPELIER PUBLISHING

Front cover images: Sally Ride becomes the first American woman in space on 18 June. *Star Wars: Return of the Jedi* is released on 25 May. The pound coin is first issued in the UK on 21 April. TV-am begins broadcasting in the UK on 1 February. The *Mario Brothers* arcade game is launched on 15 July. The Tandy 2000 PC is launched on 30 November. The Austin Maestro is launched on 1 March.

Back cover images: Sylvester Stallone is immortalised at Mann's Chinese Theater on 30 June. *Time* magazine's Men of the Year 1983 are announced on 26 December: US President Ronald Reagan and Soviet Premier Yuri Andropov. The Motorola Dynatac 8000X, the first commercial mobile phone, goes into use on 13 October. The US Strategic Defense Initiative, 'Star Wars' begins on 23 March. Jim Henson's *Fraggle Rock* is first broadcast on 10 January. *Monty Python's Meaning of Life* is first shown on 31 March.

Published in Great Britain by Montpelier Publishing.
Printed and distributed by Amazon KDP.
This edition © 2022. All rights reserved.

ISBN: 9798367259292

JANUARY 1983

Saturday 1: The foundations of the modern internet are laid as the old ARPANET computer network migrates to TCP/IP (The Internet Protocol Suite).

The term 'British subject' is officially replaced with 'British citizen' or 'Commonwealth citizen' as the British Nationality Act 1981 comes into force.

Sunday 2: The musical *Annie* closes in New York City after 2377 performances.

Monday 3: Children's ITV (CITV) is launched to compete with BBC TV's afternoon children's programmes.

Tuesday 4: The Eurythmics release their second album, *Sweet Dreams (Are Made Of This)*.

A DeLorean 'gull wing' sports car: the company goes bankrupt on 4 January.

JANUARY 1983

North Korean leader Kim Jong-un is born on 8 January.

The DeLorean Motor company of Northern Ireland, makers of the famous sports car featured in the film *Back to the Future*, files for bankruptcy in the USA.

Wednesday 5: Three police officers drown attempting unsuccessfully to save a man and his dog washed into the sea at Blackpool, Lancashire.

Thursday 6: A Danish sea captain is arrested by the Royal Navy off the Shetland Islands as 100 Danish fishing vessels break a ban on entering UK waters.

Friday 7: Australia's cricket team regain The Ashes after winning the Fifth Test against England in Sydney.

Saturday 8: Kim Jong-un, the Supreme Leader of North Korea, is born in Pyongyang, North Korea.

Sunday 9: Britain's Prime Minister Margaret Thatcher visits the Falkland Islands.

Monday 10: Jim Henson's TV puppet show for children, *Fraggle Rock*, is first broadcast.

Tuesday 11: Billy Martin becomes manager of the New York Yankees baseball team.

NASA stages a full dress-rehearsal for the launch of the Space Shuttle Challenger in February.

Fraggle Rock **is first shown on 10 January.**

Wednesday 12: The BBC reports a police crackdown on 'video piracy', the illegal copying and sale of video cassettes, which it

JANUARY 1983

describes as 'one of London's fastest growing crimes.'

Thursday 13: Seven members of a religious doomsday cult in Memphis, Tennessee are killed in a shoot-out with police following the kidnap of a patrolman two days earlier.

Friday 14: Stephen Waldorf, 26, is shot and then badly beaten by police in Earl's Court, London W8 after he is mistaken for an armed escaped convict, David Martin. Mr Waldorf eventually receives £150,000 in compensation from the Metropolitan Police.

Saturday 15: The US organised crime boss Meyer Lansksy, known as the 'mob's accountant' dies aged 80.

Australian band Men at Work top the UK charts on 15 January.

The single *Down Under* by Australian group Men at Work hits number one in the UK charts.

Sunday 16: A county court judge, William Doyle, 56, is shot dead by IRA terrorists as he leaves church in Belfast.

Monday 17: Breakfast TV is launched in the UK with the first broadcast of *BBC Breakfast Time*, presented by Frank Bough, Selina Scott and Nick Ross.

Tuesday 18: Israeli and Lebanese negotiators announce they have made 'good progress' in peace talks to end the 35-year long state of war between their two countries.

Nazi fugitive Klaus Barbie (shown here in 1941) is captured on 19 January.

Wednesday 19: The high-ranking Nazi fugitive Klaus Barbie is arrested in

JANUARY 1983

Tennis champ Björn Borg announces his retirement on 23 January.

Bolivia; he later stands trial for war crimes carried out in occupied France during the Second World War.

Thursday 20: FBI agents shoot dead a hijacker holding 41 people hostage on a Northwest Orient jet liner at Seattle, Washington. The suspect, Glen Tripp, 20, was on probation for a previous hijacking attempt in 1980.

Friday 21: Surtitles (subtitles which appear above the stage of a theatre) are first used, during a production of the opera *Elektra* in Toronto, Canada.

Saturday 22: Leonard Nimoy (Mr Spock in *Star Trek*) announces he will direct the third *Star Trek* film, *The Search for Spock.*

Sunday 23: The US TV action series *The A Team* is first broadcast.

Tennis champion Björn Borg announces his retirement.

The ban on foreign boats fishing in British waters is lifted as the EEC's Common Fisheries Policy comes into effect.

Monday 24: A Soviet satellite, out of control for over a month, crashes harmlessly into the Indian Ocean, ending fears that it might hit a populated area.

25 members of the terrorist group the Red Brigade are sentenced to life imprisonment for the killing of the Italian politician Aldo Mori in 1978.

Tuesday 25: The Infrared Astronomical Satellite, a joint US/Netherlands/UK observatory, is launched.

Wednesday 26: Red rain falls on the UK, caused by sand from the Sahara Desert being taken up into the atmosphere.

Thursday 27: Former Beatle George Harrison announces he no

JANUARY 1983

onger wishes to be known solely for his time with the band, saying 'we were all just a bunch of loonies'.

Friday 28: David Martin, the dangerous escaped convict whom London police thought they had found on 14 January when they accidentally shot Stephen Waldorf, is arrested after a dramatic chase through the tunnels in Hampstead underground station.

Saturday 29: All 60 members of Indira Gandhi's Indian cabinet resign in an attempt to restore flagging confidence in the ruling Congress Party.

Sunday 30: The Washington Redskins beat the Miami Dolphins 27-17 in the 27th Superbowl American football championships in Pasadena, California.

Monday 31: The wearing of seatbelts for car drivers and front seat passengers becomes compulsory in the UK.

British government propaganda advertising the new seatbelt law introduced on 31 January, with the slogan 'clunk-click', the sound of a seatbelt being fastened.

FEBRUARY 1983

Tuesday 1: Britain's second breakfast television service, TV-AM, goes into operation.

Wednesday 2: One of the most prolific bigamists of all time, Giovanni Vigliotto of Phoenix, Arizona, goes on trial for contracting 105 bigamous marriages.

Thursday 3: Unemployment in the UK stands at a record high of 3,224,715.

Friday 4: Scott Hamilton and Rosalyn Summers win the US figure skating championships.

Saturday 5: The former high-ranking Nazi Klaus Barbie is brought to trial.

Left: TV-AM begins broadcasting on 1 February. Presenters include fitness guru 'Mad' Lizzie Webb.

FEBRUARY 1983

House of Horror: on 10 February serial killer Dennis Nilsen is arrested on suspicion of multiple murders in the attic flat of a house in the genteel north London suburb of Muswell Hill.

20 people are killed when a car bomb explodes outside the Libyan Embassy in Beirut, Lebanon.

Sunday 6: Jim Ameche, brother of actor Don Ameche and star of the long-running US radio serial *Jack Armstrong: the All American Boy*, dies aged 67.

Monday 7: It is revealed that the Nazi fugitive Klaus Barbie was an informer for US military intelligence after the Second World War.

Tuesday 8: The champion racehorse Shergar is stolen from his stable in County Kildare. The kidnappers, most likely members of the provisional IRA, demand a £2m ransom, which is not paid. Despite an extensive investigation, the horse is never found.

The song and dance show for children, *Minipops*, is first broadcast on the Channel 4 in the UK. It is later dropped after criticism of its alleged sexualisation of youngsters.

Wednesday 9: The government of North Vietnam officially denies rumours that it is still holding American prisoners of war captive, ten years after the end of US military involvement in the region.

Thursday 10: A 37 year old civil servant, Dennis Nilsen, is charged with murder after body parts are found at his home in Cranley Gardens, London N10. Further investigations reveal that

FEBRUARY 1983

Above: Michael Jackson hits number one in the UK charts on 12 February.

Nilsen has murdered at least 12 young men, making him one of the most notorious serial killers in British history.

Friday 11: The Rolling Stones film *Let's Spend the Night Together* is released.

The US envoy to the Middle East, Philip Habib, announces a peace plan for the withdrawal of Syrian, Israeli and Palestinian forces from the Lebanon.

Saturday 12: Additional tests are announced for the troubled Space Shuttle *Challenger*, whose maiden flight is delayed due to technical problems.

Billie Jean by Michael Jackson hits number one in the UK singles chart.

Sunday 13: Comedian Jerry Lewis marries dancer Sandee Pitnick.

Two US Marshals are killed in a shoot out in Medina, North Dakota, with Gordon Kahl, leader of the Posse Comitatus extremist group.

Small wonder: the Austin Metro becomes Britain's best-selling car on 15 February.

FEBRUARY 1983

Monday 14: General Motors and Toyota agree to produce a new small US-Japanese car in California.

Dino de Lorean and Barbara Kane set a world record for continuous kissing, smooching for five days and twelve hours in a shop window in Los Angeles, California.

Tuesday 15: The Austin Metro becomes Britain's most popular car, outselling every other make registered in January.

Wednesday 16: (Ash Wednesday). 75 people are killed in some of the worst bushfires in Australian history.

Vladimir Salnikov sets a swimming record on 19 February.

Thursday 17: The Lebanese government bans Israeli forces from most of East Beirut as tensions rise between Israeli and Lebanese peacekeeping troops.

The Queen and Prince Philip begin a five day tour of Mexico.

Friday 18: At least 2000 people are killed in a sectarian uprising in Assam, India.

Saturday 19: Russian swimmer Vladimir Salnikov sets the record for the men's 400m freestyle at 3.48.32 in Moscow, USSR.

13 people are killed in a gangland shoot-out in Seattle, Washington, the worst in the city's history.

Sunday 20: The US army reverses a ban on slot machines on its bases. One-armed bandits were removed in 1972 from all military installations following widespread cheating.

Willie Nelson wins a Grammy Award on 23 February.

FEBRUARY 1983

Monday 21: Donald Davies sets the world record for running a mile backwards at 6 minutes 7 seconds at the University of Hawaii.

Tuesday 22: The prominent British conductor Sir Adrian Boult dies aged 93.

Wednesday 23: In the 25th Grammy Awards held in Los Angeles, *Rosanna* by Toto wins Record of the Year, Willie Nelson's *Always On My Mind* wins Song of the Year and Australian band Men at Work win Best New Artist.

Thursday 24: A by-election takes place in Bermondsey, London, notable for two reasons. It sees the largest by-election swing in British history (44.2%) when Simon Hughes (Liberal) defeats Peter Tatchell (Labour), and is also the first election contested by the newly formed Monster Raving Loony Party headed by Screaming Lord Sutch.

Eccentric politician Screaming Lord Sutch (in top hat) fights his first election on 24 February.

Friday 25: The playwright Tennessee Williams (*A Streetcar Named Desire*) dies aged 71.

Saturday 26: HM Queen Elizabeth II and HRH Prince Philip begin a tour of California.

Michael Jackson's *Thriller* album hits number one in the US charts where it remains for 37 weeks.

Sunday 27: Peter Bird (GB), the first man to row across the Pacific Ocean singlehandedly, meets another human for the first time since August 1982 during a scheduled supply-drop off near Tahiti.

Monday 28: The final episode of the TV series *M*A*S*H* is broadcast in the USA, watched by a record 125 million people.

MARCH 1983

Tuesday 1: British Leyland launches the Austin Maestro, a replacement for the Allegro and Maxi, featuring an advanced voice synthesiser warning system.

HM Queen Elizabeth II and Prince Philip meet US President Ronald Reagan and his wife Nancy in California.

Wednesday 2: The first Compact Discs are launched in the USA, UK and Europe.

Thursday 3: The Belgian cartoonist Hergé (Georges Remi), the creator of Tintin, dies aged 75.

Friday 4: The actor Harrison Ford marries screenwriter Melissa Mathison.

The Austin Maestro is launched on 1 March.

MARCH 1983

Saturday 5: Bob Hawke's Labor party defeats Malcolm Fraser's Liberals in the Australian general election.

Pope John Paul II visits Panama.

Sunday 6: Helmut Kohl is swept to victory as Chancellor in the West German federal election, as the incumbent Social Democrats experience their worst defeat in 30 years.

Monday 7: The Queen and Prince Philip conclude their tour of the US west coast, departing for Canada from Seattle, Washington.

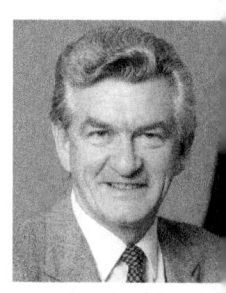

Bob Hawke becomes PM of Australia on 5 March.

Tuesday 8: IBM releases its second personal computer, the IBM PC XT.

US President Ronald Reagan coins the phrase 'evil empire' to describe the USSR, in a speech to the National Association of Evangelicals in Florida.

The British composer Sir William Walton, famous for his Crown Imperial march for the coronation of HM Queen Elizabeth II, dies aged 80.

Wednesday 9: Chuck Hull of 3D Systems of Rock Hill, South Carolina, invents the first prototype 3D printer.

The US National Music Publishers' Association awards John Williams' theme from *ET* as best movie theme of the year.

Thursday 10: Donald Maclean, a member of the infamous

HM the Queen and Prince Philip meet President and Mrs Reagan on 1 March.

MARCH 1983

Cambridge ring of traitors who spied for the Soviets in the 1950s, dies aged 69 in exile in the USSR.

Friday 11: Jayne Torvill and Christopher Dean (GB) win the Ice Dance Championship in Helsinki, Finland.

Saturday 12: Don Ritchie (GB) sets the world record for running 50 miles at 4.51.49 at Copthall Stadium, London.

The IBM PC XT is released on 8 March.

Sunday 13: The musical *Woman of the Year* starring Lauren Bacall closes on Broadway after 770 performances.

Joshua Nkomo, opposition leader of Zimbabwe, flees to London after a falling out with the country's ruler, Robert Mugabe.

Monday 14: Following fears of a price war due to reduced demand for oil, the OPEC cartel cuts the price of a barrel of oil from $34 to $29, the first such reduction in 22 years.

Tuesday 15: The writer and literary critic Dame Rebecca West DBE dies aged 90.

The actress Barbara Bel Geddes (Miss Ellie in *Dallas*) undergoes a quadruple bypass after suffering a heart attack.

Joshua Nkomo flees Zimbabwe on 13 March.

Wednesday 16: Two Israeli soldiers are killed and five US Marines wounded in a grenade attack on peacekeeping forces in Beirut, Lebanon.

A group of Japanese-Americans begins a class action suit against the US government seeking reparations of $24bn over their internment during the Second World War.

MARCH 1983

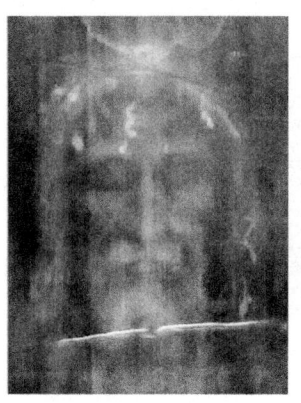

King Umberto II, last monarch of Italy (left), dies on 18 March; two days later it is announced he has bequeathed the Turin Shroud (far left) to the Vatican.

The shroud is said to bear the imprint of Christ's face after it was used to wrap His body.

Thursday 17: TRH Prince Charles and Princess Diana with their 9 month old son Prince William begin a six week tour of Australia and New Zealand.

Friday 18: Umberto II, last king of Italy, dies in exile in Switzerland aged 78.

Saturday 19: France and Ireland finish level on points in Rugby's Five Nations finals; since no tie-break procedure exists they are declared joint winners.

Sunday 20: The playwright Arthur Miller arrives in Peking to begin directing a Chinese version of his play, *Death of a Salesman.*

Larry Holmes becomes World Heavyweight champion on 27 March.

It is announced that His late Majesty King Umberto II, exiled king of Italy, bequeathed the Turin Shroud to the Vatican.

Monday 21: The Ivory Coast changes its capital from Abidjan to Yamousoukro.

The only typographical error to have appeared on the cover of *Time* magazine appears on this date's issue; all copies are recalled.

Tuesday 22: Chaim Herzog is elected as President of Israel.

MARCH 1983

Above: the Strategic Defense Initiative ('Star Wars') is launched on 23 March.

Wednesday 23: US President Ronald Reagan announces his 'Star Wars' programme (the Strategic Defense Initiative), a defence system capable of shooting down Soviet missiles.

Mr Barney Clark, 62, of Salt Lake City, Utah, first recipient of an artificial heart 112 days previously, dies from an unrelated illness; his heart and circulation remain working after his death.

Thursday 24: Nicaraguan troops clash with forces from neighbouring Honduras in a border skirmish 180 miles north of the capital Managua.

Friday 25: The Russian speed skater Pavel Pegov sets two world records on the same day at the Medeu stadium in Almaty, USSR; the 500m (36.68s) and the 1000m (1m 12.58s). At the same event East Germany's Christa Luding-Rothenburger sets the women's 500m record at 39.69s.

Saturday 26: Liverpool wins the Football League Cup for the third successive year, beating Manchester United 2-1 at Wembley Stadium, London.

Sunday 27: Larry Holmes beats Lucien Rodriguez to win the World Heavyweight boxing title in Scranton, Pennsylvania.

Monday 28: Ian McGregor is appointed head of Britain's National Coal Board.

Giovanni Vigliotto, 53, is sentenced to 34 years in prison by a judge in Phoenix, Arizona, for contracting 105 bigamous marriages.

Love machine: Giovanni Vigliotto is sentenced on 28 March for 105 counts of bigamy.

MARCH 1983

Tuesday 29: The UK Parliament debates the privatisation of British Telecom, a matter of much discussion and opposition since its announcement in 1982. Shares eventually go on sale in 1984.

Wednesday 30: The Ray Cooney farce *Run for Your Wife* starring Richard Briers and Bernard Cribbins opens in London's West End.

Thursday 31: The film Monty Python's *Meaning of Life* is released in the USA.

Above: poster for the Monty Python film *The Meaning of Life*, released on 31 March.

APRIL 1983

Above: the Vauxhall Nova is launched in Britain on 1 April.

Herve Villechaize announces he is leaving *Fantasy Island* on 1 April.

Friday 1: (Good Friday) The Vauxhall Nova small car is launched in the UK, replacing the Chevette.

Thousands of protesters form a 14 mile human chain in opposition to the siting of US nuclear weapons in Britain.

Herve Villechaize, who plays Tattoo in the TV series *Fantasy Island*, announces he is leaving the show.

Saturday 2: Sir Richard Attenborough is awarded the *Padma Bushan,* India's third highest civilian award, for producing and directing the film *Gandhi*.

Sunday 3: (Easter Sunday) The Reverend Robert Cromey, a priest in San Francisco, is barred at the last minute by his bishop from performing the planned first blessing of a same-sex relationship in the US Episcopal (Anglican) church.

APRIL 1983

Challenger makes its maiden voyage on 4 April.

Monday 4: The Space Shuttle *Challenger* is launched on its maiden voyage.

Hollywood golden age star Gloria Swanson dies aged 84.

Tuesday 5: The biggest robbery in British history to this date takes place when an armed gang escape with £7m after raiding the Security Express headquarters in Shoreditch, east London.

Wednesday 6: David Frost, host of the new TV-Am breakfast show on British TV, loses his job in a move by management to make the show less 'metropolitan'.

Thursday 7: 20,000 people are forced to flee their homes as major flooding hits the US state of Louisiana.

Astronauts from the Space Shuttle *Challenger* make the first US spacewalk in nine years.

David Frost is sacked from TV-Am on 6 April.

Chrisopher Warwick's biography of HRH Princess Margaret is published.

APRIL 1983

Friday 8: One of the oldest humanoid skeletons found to this date, that of a Neanderthal who died c.78,000BC, is discovered in Egypt.

Saturday 9: The first *Challenger* space shuttle mission ends successfully as the reuseable craft returns to earth.

Sunday 10: In a TV address US President Ronald Reagan outlines tax cuts, going against the previous Democrat policy which he describes as 'America makes; government takes.'

The film *ET* wins four Oscars on 11 April.

Senior Palestinian Liberation Organisation (PLO) member Issam Sartawi is assassinated.

Monday 11: Richard Attenborough's film *Gandhi* wins eight Academy Awards; Stephen Spielberg's *ET: The Extra Terrestrial* wins four.

Seve Ballesteros of Spain wins the PGA golf Masters Tournament.

Tuesday 12: Britain's Parliament debates the proposed Youth Training Scheme (YTS) designed to provide employment for school leavers. The scheme is later criticised for exploiting workers by paying them low wages.

Wednesday 13: US President Ronald Reagan denies that he is involved in secret negotiations to overthrow Nicaragua's Sandinista government.

An eight-storey high inflatable replica of a gorilla is attached to the Empire State Building in New York City to celebrate the fiftieth anniversary of the film *King Kong*. The stunt is cut short on Monday when the balloon springs a leak and has to be removed.

Thursday 14: Research published in the *New England Journal of Medicine* suggests a link between the contraceptive pill and an increase in certain forms of heart disease.

APRIL 1983

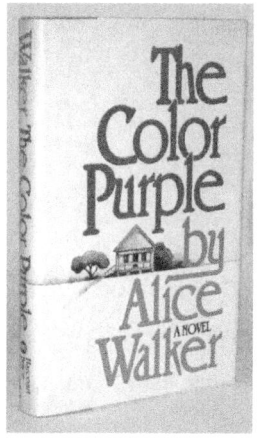

Richard Attenborough refuses to attend a whites-only showing of his film *Gandhi* when it premieres in Johannesburg, South Africa.

Friday 15: The Roman Catholic Church holds its 17th World Communications Day, in which Pope John Paul II urges journalists to be workers for peace and the common good.

Police in Poland carry out nationwide mass arrests of members of the anti-communist Solidarity movement, as well as seizing printing presses and radio transmitters.

The Color Purple **wins the Pulitzer Prize on 19 April.**

Saturday 16: Baseball player Steve Garvey of the San Diego Padres breaks the record of appearing in consecutive games (1118). He continues until he has reached 1207 games in July.

Sunday 17: Fighting intensifies on the Sino-Vietnamese border in response to what China claims are 'armed provocations' from neighbouring Vietnamese forces.

Monday 18: 63 die when Islamic fundamentalists bomb the US Embassy in Beirut, Lebanon. It is the deadliest attack on an American diplomatic mission to this date.

The one pound coin is introduced in England and Wales on 21 April. Promotional wallets containing the coins are issued by many companies such as Ty-Phoo Tea (above).

APRIL 1983

Marines search the ruins of the US Embassy in Beirut, which is bombed on 17 April.

Tuesday 19: *The Color Purple* by Alice Walker wins the 1983 Pulitzer Prize for Literature.

Wednesday 20: US President Reagan signs a $165bn bail-out for America's troubled social security system.

The USSR launches the Soyuz T-8 space mission.

Thursday 21: The one pound coin is introduced in England and Wales, as an alternative to the pound note. Pound notes remain in circulation in England and Wales until 1988 but continue in a limited number in Scotland to the present day.

Friday 22: The jazz pianist and big-band leader Earl 'Fatha' Hines dies aged 79.

The German magazine *Stern* announces it has discovered diaries by Adolf Hitler; they are later proven to be fakes.

Saturday 23: Corinne Hermes of Luxembourg wins the Eurovision Song Contest with *Si La Vie Est Cadeau.*

The Olympic swimmer and actor Buster Crabbe, famous for his roles as Flash Gordon, Buck Rogers and Tarzan, dies aged 75.

APRIL 1983

Blues legend Muddy Waters dies on 30 April.

Sunday 24: The West German Formula One driver Rolf Stommelen is killed in a crash during the *Los Angeles Times* Grand Prix in Riverside, California.

Monday 25: The NASA space probe Pioneer 10 passes Pluto.

The British historian David Irving is ejected from a press conference held by *Stern* magazine after he raises concerns that the Hitler Diaries they intend to publish may be forgeries.

Tuesday 26: A ten year old girl, Samantha Smith of Manchester, Maine, hits the headlines when she receives a personal reply to a letter she sent to Soviet premier Yuri Andropov asking why he wanted war with the USA. Andropov assures her he is a man of peace and invites her to visit the USSR, which she accepts.

Wednesday 27: Nolan Ryan of the Houston Astros makes baseball history when he achieves a career record of 3509 strike-outs.

Michael Fagan, the mentally ill man who broke into the Queen's bedroom in 1982, is boo'd off stage while attempting to make a punk rock singing debut in London's Son of Batcave club.

Thursday 28: West Germany's *Stern* magazine publishes the Hitler Diaries, despite concerns from historians that they may not be genuine.

Friday 29: Harold Washington becomes Chicago's first black mayor.

Saturday 30: Blues singer Muddy Waters dies aged 68.

True by Spandau Ballet hits number one in the UK singles charts.

MAY 1983

Sunday 1: A rocket attack takes place on the US ambassador's residence in Beirut, Lebanon; the missiles fall short without causing damage.

Large protests take place across Poland, organised by the anti-communist Solidarity movement under Lech Walesa.

President Ronald Reagan is voted the USA's best dressed man in the Fashion Foundation of America Awards. Actor Dustin Hoffman also receives an award – for being the best dressed man in woman's clothing following his role in the film *Tootsie*.

Monday 2: NASA scientists begin a delicate remote operation using booster rockets to move the Tracking and Data Relay Satellite, misplaced by the Space Shuttle *Challenger*, into its correct orbit.

Tuesday 3: New Order release their second album, *Power, Corruption & Lies.*

Wednesday 4: Five Royal Navy destroyers are sent to boost the Falkland Islands' defences after rumours of a renewed Argentinian attack on the British colony.

Comedian George Burns reveals his secrets of longevity on 5 May in *How to Live to 100*.

MAY 1983

Widespread damage is caused and hundreds injured when an earthquake hits Coalinga, California.

Thursday 5: Comedian George Burns, 87, publishes a book entitled *How to Live to 100*. He reaches the target in 1996, dying shortly afterwards.

Friday 6: The West German government announces that after forensic examination, the Hitler Diaries published by *Stern* magazine are fakes.

Konrad Kujau is arrested on 15 May on suspicion of forging Hitler's diaries.

Saturday 7: The Cold War thriller film *Wargames* is released.

Sunday 8: Speculation abounds about who forged the recently 'discovered' Hitler diaries published by *Stern* magazine. Nazi hunter Simon Weisenthal suggests they are the work of exiled Nazis in South America.

Monday 9: British Prime Minister Margaret Thatcher calls a General Election for 9 June.

Lead singer Sting (Gordon Sumner) of The Police. The band releases *Every Breath You Take* on 20 May.

Tuesday 10: The gravestone of the actor James Dean, which was stolen from a cemetery in Fairmount, Indiana on 14 April, is recovered from nearby woodland.

Wednesday 11: Aberdeen FC beats Real Madrid 2-1 to win the European Cup Winners' Cup.

Thursday 12: Julie Lynne Hayek is crowned Miss USA.

Friday 13: US President Ronald Reagan issues a

MAY 1983

pardon for Eugenio Martinez, one of the conspirators in the 1974 Watergate scandal.

Saturday 14: Dundee United FC beat Dundee FC to win the Scottish Premier Division for the first time in the club's history.

The Human League's single *Keep Feeling Fascination* reaches its peak at number two in the UK charts.

Sunday 15: Konrad Kujau, 44, a dealer in Nazi regalia, is arrested in Frankfurt on suspicion of having forged the recently published Hitler Diaries.

Monday 16: The Lebanese government agrees to Israel's proposal to withdraw 25,000 of its troops from the Lebanon. Wheel clamps are first used in London to prevent illegal parking.

Tuesday 17: An Israeli-American accord is signed, agreeing that Israel has the right of self-defence against attacks by Lebanese terrorists.

Wednesday 18: Peter Bird, the British rower attempting a solo crossing of the Pacific Ocean, is reported as being 860 miles from Australia.

Thursday 19: *Star Trek* actor William Shatner is honoured with a pavement star on Hollywood Boulevard.

The Japanese film *Narayama Bushiko* wins the Palme d'Or at the Cannes Film Festival.

Friday 20: The Police release their single *Every Breath You Take*, which goes on to be voted Billboard magazine's Song of the Year 1983.

William Shatner joins Hollywood's legends on 19 May.

Larry Holmes retains his World Heavyweight Boxing champion title after beating Tim Witherspoon in Las Vegas.

MAY 1983

The journal *Science* publishes two studies outlining a new virus known as HIV/AIDS.

Saturday 21: David Bowie's single *Let's Dance* hits number one in the US charts.

Manchester United draw 2-2 with Brighton and Hove Albion in the FA Cup Final at Wembley Stadium, London.

The historian Kenneth Clark (Lord Clark) dies aged 79.

Sunday 22: The US government issues a condemnation of Iran's persecution of adherents of the Ba'hai religion.

Monday 23: The USSR's English-language broadcaster Vladimir Danchev is taken off the air after authorities learn from the BBC that he has changed scripts to include anti-Soviet propaganda.

Tuesday 24: Fred Sinowatz becomes Chancellor of Austria.

Wednesday 25: The third Star Wars film, *Return of the Jedi,* is released.

Thursday 26: 100 die when a major earthquake and tsunami hit Honshu, Japan.

Manchester United defeats Brighton and Hove Albion 4-0 in the replay of the 1983 FA Cup Final.

Friday 27: 11 die in an explosion at an illegal fireworks factory in Benton, Tennessee.

Saturday 28: The ninth G7 trade summit opens in Williamsburg, Virginia.

Sunday 29: Yuri Dumchev of the USSR sets the world discus throwing record at 235' 9" (71.86m).

Monday 30: In county cricket, Surrey has its worst ever result (14 all out) against Essex in Chelmsford.

Tuesday 31: The former US World Heavyweight boxing champion (1919-26) Jack Dempsey dies aged 86.

JUNE 1983

Wednesday 1: Lester Piggott wins the Epsom Derby on Teenoso.

Bette Davis wins the Charles Chaplin Award for lifetime achievement in films.

Thursday 2: 23 die when an Air Canada DC-9 airliner catches fire mid-flight and crash lands at Cinncinnati, Ohio.

Friday 3: The remains of 9 US servicemen killed in the Vietnam War are handed over to an American team in Hanoi. Several thousand servicemen are still listed to this date as missing, presumed dead, in the conflict, in which US involvement ended in 1973.

San Francisco institutes the USA's harshest anti-smoking policies to this date, requiring all offices to have separate smoking and non-smoking areas.

Bette Davis wins a lifetime award on 1 June.

Saturday 4: Chris Evert (USA) defeats Mima Jausovec (Yugoslavia) to win the women's French Open tennis tournament.

Every Breath You Take by The Police hits number one in the UK singles charts.

JUNE 1983

Sunday 5: The Andrew Lloyd Webber show *Cats* wins Best Musical in the 37th Tony Awards held in New York City.

Yannick Noah (France) wins the men's French Open tennis tournament.

Monday 6: The 13th James Bond film, *Octopussy*, premieres, starring Roger Moore, Maud Adams and Louis Jourdan.

Tuesday 7: Nazi war criminal Heinz Barth, an SS officer complicit in the massacre of 734 civilians in the Second World War, is sentenced to life imprisonment by a court in Berlin, East Germany.

Roger Moore stars in *Octopussy*, which premieres on 6 June.

Wednesday 8: The comedy film *Trading Places*, starring Dan Ackroyd and Eddie Murphy, is released.

Thursday 9: The Conservative party under Margaret Thatcher wins a landslide victory in Britain's general election. The election also sees the retirement of former Prime Minister Harold Wilson as an MP.

Friday 10: The inventor and computer scientist Clive Sinclair is knighted.

Saturday 11: Zhu Jianhua of China sets the high jump world record at 7' 9'5" (2.38m) in Peking.

Margaret Thatcher's Conservative party is re-elected in a landslide victory on 9 June.

Sunday 12: Following the Conservative party election victory of 9 June, Michael Foot resigns as leader of the Labour party and HM Opposition.

JUNE 1983

Monday 13: The space probe Pioneer 10 becomes the first man-made object to leave the Solar System.

Tuesday 14: Roy Jenkins resigns as leader of Britain's Social Democratic Party (SDP) and is succeeded by David Owen.

Wednesday 15: The BBC TV sitcom *Blackadder* is first broadcast.

Thursday 16: The National Museum of Photography, Film and Television opens in Bradford.

Sally Ride becomes the first American woman in space on 18 June.

Hundreds of thousands of people turn out to greet Pope John Paul II when he visits his homeland of Poland.

Friday 17: 425 people are arrested in a nationwide crackdown on organised crime in Italy. Suspects include a priest, a nun and a popular TV game show host.

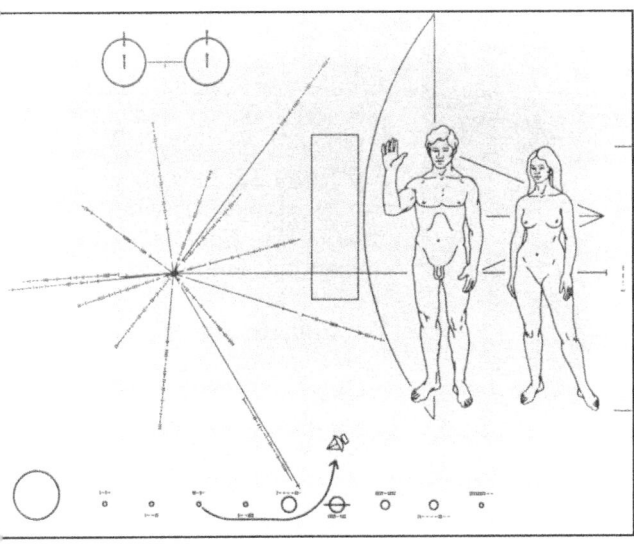

Pioneer 10 leaves the solar system on 13 June. Attached is an image (left) intended to inform intelligent alien life about humans and the planet Earth.

JUNE 1983

Saturday 18: Nine women, including a teenager, are hanged in Shiraz, Iran, because of their adherence to the Baha'i religion.

The second *Challenger* Space Shuttle mission is launched; Sally Ride becomes the first American woman in space.

Sunday 19: The 24 Hours of Le Mans motor race is won by a US team led by Vern Schuppan.

Monday 20: *Newsweek* magazine states that the British government has given up hope of retaining sovereignty over Hong Kong Island after the lease on its mainland Chinese territory expires in 1997.

Tuesday 21: Up to 40 are killed in clashes between Lebanese rebel guerillas and Palestine Liberation Organisation (PLO) forces in eastern Lebanon.

Wednesday 22: A satellite is retrieved from orbit and then replaced using the Space Shuttle Challenger's robot arm, as a practice run for future 'search and rescue' missions to damaged space hardware.

Thursday 23: Lech Walesa, the leader of the anti-communist Solidarity movement meets Pope John Paul II in Poland.

The Space Shuttle robot arm is first used on 22 June.

Friday 24: The second *Challenger* Space Shuttle mission ends.

Saturday 25: India wins the Cricket World Cup when it defeats the West Indies 183:140 at Lord's, London.

Sunday 26: Thousands flee their homes as heavy rainfall causes the Colorado River to flood after reaching its highest level since 1908.

JUNE 1983

Monday 27: The *Challenger* Space Shuttle crew begins the shortest ever debriefing (4.5 days as opposed to an average of three weeks) in US space flight history, due to an uneventful mission.

Tuesday 28: The geostationary satellite Galaxy 1 is launched.

Wednesday 29: The US government steps up investigations into servicemen who went missing in action during the Vietnam War, after reports surface in Thailand of POWs still being held by communist forces.

Thursday 30: Hollywood star Sylvester Stallone has his hand and foot prints cast in cement at Mann's Chinese Theater in Los Angeles.

William Shatner is awarded Best Actor in the Saturn Awards for Science Fiction.

JULY 1983

Friday 1: 23 die when a North Korean airliner crashes in Guinea-Bissau.

The US architect R Buckminster Fuller, inventor of the geodesic dome, dies aged 87.

Saturday 2: John McEnroe (USA) wins the men's singles tennis tournament at Wimbledon when he beats Chris Lewis of New Zealand 6-2, 6-2, 6-2.

Sunday 3: The world's biggest bingo contest takes place on the Cherokee Reservation in North Carolina. Over US$1m in prizes are awarded with a jackpot of $200,000.

John McEnroe (far left) beats Chris Lewis at Wimbledon on 2 July.

JULY 1983

Right: American schoolgirl Samantha Smith (with bag) attends a Soviet youth camp on her tour of the USSR which starts on 7 July.

Monday 4: Soviet violinist Victoria Mullova, 23, defects to the west after a concert in Finland, leaving behind a priceless Stradivarius violin in her hotel room.

Tuesday 5: The big-band leader and trumpet player Harry James, wife of Hollywood star Betty Grable, dies aged 67.

Wednesday 6: US Vice-President George Bush announces that Ronald Reagan will run for President again in the 1984 elections.

Thursday 7: Britain's Chancellor of the Exchequer announces spending cuts of £500m.

Samantha Smith, the American schoolgirl who wrote to Soviet premier Andropov urging him to make peace with the USA, begins a tour of the USSR.

Friday 8: The World Scout Jamboree takes place in Alberta, Canada; it is the first Jamboree that girls are permitted to attend.

Mehmet Ali Agca, who attempted to assassinate Pope John Paul II in 1981, alleges from prison that he was acting under orders from the Soviet secret police, the KGB.

Saturday 9: The National Women's Political Caucus urges US President Ronald Reagan not to stand for re-election due to his 'hopeless' record on womens' rights.

JULY 1983

Joe Tong sets the record for the fastest crossing of the USA in an ultralight aircraft (weighing just 250lb) at 18 days.

Sunday 10: The Israeli government bans the formation of citizens' militias in the West Bank, as settlers demand greater protection after a spate of Arab attacks.

Monday 11: The pulp detective story writer Ross Macdonald dies aged 67.

Lorraine Downes, 19, is crowned Miss Universe.

119 die in an airliner crash near Cuenca, Ecuador; it is the country's worst air disaster to this date.

Lorraine Downes becomes Miss Universe on 11 July.

Tuesday 12: Moscow indicates that it is willing to loosen restrictions on the emigration of political and religious dissidents, including 'refuseniks' (Jews who wish to emigrate to Israel).

Wednesday 13: Neil Kinnock, future leader of the Labour Party and HM Opposition, escapes serious injury when his car overturns on the M4 motorway.

Thursday 14: The Japanese games company Nintendo releases *Mario Brothers*.

Friday 15: Armenian terrorists kill 8 people and injure 55 in a bomb attack on the Turkish Airlines desk at Orly Airport, Paris.

Saturday 16: 20 die when a British Airways Sikorsky passenger helicopter crashes in bad weather en route from Cornwall to the Isles of Scilly.

The Mario Brothers arcade game is launched on 14 July.

JULY 1983

Pilot Dick Smith takes a break on Baffin Island from the first round the world helicopter trip, which he finishes on 22 July.

Sunday 17: Tom Watson (USA) wins his fifth British Open Golf tournament at Royal Birkdale, Merseyside.

Monday 18: Samantha Smith, the US schoolgirl invited on a tour of the Soviet Union, meets Valentina Tereshkova, the first woman in space.

Tuesday 19: London's Natural History Museum unveils a huge skeleton of a previously unknown species of dinosaur similar to a Megalosaurus. The skeleton, described by the museum as 'the find of the century' was discovered in Surrey by amateur fossil hunter Bill Walker, 55.

Wednesday 20: The government of Poland announces the end of martial law and an amnesty for political prisoners.

Thursday 21: Britain's former Prime Minister Harold Wilson is awarded a life peerage, becoming Baron Wilson of Rievaulx.

The lowest temperature on Earth is recorded at Vostok, Antarctica. (-128.6F/-89.2C).

Friday 22: Dick Smith of Australia completes the first global circumnavigation by helicopter.

JULY 1983

Production of the Ford Orion begins in the UK.

Production of the Ford Orion begins on 22 July.

Saturday 23: The Sri Lankan Civil War begins.

Wherever I Lay My Hat by Paul Young hits UK number one.

Sunday 24: Rioting breaks out between rival Tamil and Sinhalese ethnic groups in Sri Lanka.

Monday 25: Metallica's debut album *Kill 'Em All* is released.

Tuesday 26: A Roman Catholic mother of ten, Victoria Gillick, loses her case in the High Court to prevent the distribution of contraceptives to under 16s in England without parental consent.

Veteran actor David Niven dies on 29 July.

Yiu Nam Chiu, a Hong Kong merchant seaman and member of the Royal Fleet Auxiliary is awarded the George Cross for rescuing Royal Navy personnel from the crippled ship *Sir Galahad* in June 1982 during the Falklands War.

Wednesday 27: Seven die in an Armenian terrorist attack on the Turkish Embassy in Lisbon, Portugal.

Kill 'Em All is released on 25 July.

JULY 1983

Paul Young's single *Wherever I Lay My Hat* hits number one on 23 July.

Thursday 28: The future Russian President Vladimir Putin marries flight attendant Lyudmila Shkrebneva.

Friday 29: The actor David Niven dies aged 73; actor Raymond Massey dies aged 86.

Saturday 30: Sergey Didyk sets the world weight-lifting record at 261kg (575.4 lb) in Moscow, USSR.

Sunday 31: Jan Stephenson (Australia) wins the US Open women's golf tournament at Cedar Ridge, Oklahoma.

AUGUST 1983

Monday 1: The new 'A' prefix registration numbers go into use on new UK cars. The system, which indicates the vehicle's age at the beginning rather than the end of the number, remains in use until 2001.

New Zealand has its first Test cricket victory in England, defeating the English side by five wickets at Headingley.

Tuesday 2: The situation in the Lebanon deteriorates as Israeli, Syrian, Palestinians and the Christian Militia clash in various skirmishes across the country.

Wednesday 3: British Prime Minister Margaret Thatcher undergoes surgery for a detached retina.

Thursday 4: Bettino Craxi becomes Prime Minister of Italy.

Friday 5: 22 IRA members receive sentences totalling 4,000 years from Belfast Crown Court.

Saturday 6: The US government announces military aid to the former French colony of Chad as tensions increase with neighbouring Libya.

Bettino Craxi becomes Prime Minister of Italy on 4 August.

AUGUST 1983

The historic Bishop's Palace in Trondheim, Norway, is engulfed by fire on 18 August.

Sunday 7: 35 die when a bomb explodes in a market in Baalbek in the Lebanon; nationalist guerillas are thought to be responsible.

The first World Athletics Championships begins in Helsinki, Finland.

Monday 8: Billy Joel's album *An Innocent Man* is released.

Guatemala's president Brigadier General Efrain Rios Montt is ousted in a coup by Defence Minister Oscar Victores.

Tuesday 9: 180 French paratroopers are sent to the former French colony of Chad as border skirmishes with Libya increase.

Wednesday 10: Flash flooding hits central Las Vegas, with water up to three feet deep in some areas. Twopeople are reported missing, presumed drowned; most casinos, however, remain open.

Queen Dzilewe, Queen Regent of Swaziland is forced to abdicate and is replaced by Queen Ntfombi.

Thursday 11: A partial blackout hits central New York City, with many shops, hotels and businesses forced to close.

Friday 12: Anti-clericalists set off a bomb in the shrine of

AUGUST 1983

George Michael (far left) and Andrew Ridgeley of Wham! have a top ten hit with Club Tropicana on 20 August.

Lourdes, France, in protest against a planned visit by Pope John Paul II. Nobody is injured, and somewhat ironically, the only damage caused is to a statue of Pontius Pilate.

Saturday 13: *Give It Up* by KC and the Sunshine Band hits number one in the UK singles charts.

Sunday 14: Actress Mila Kunis is born in Chernivtsi, USSR.

Pope John Paul II visits the shrine of Lourdes, France, amid tight security following the anti-clerical bomb attack of 12 August.

Monday 15: Johnny Ramone, lead singer of punk band The Ramones, is seriously injured and undergoes brain surgery after his involvement in a drunken brawl in New York City.

Tuesday 16: Paul Simon, late of Simon and Garfunkel, marries actress Carrie Fisher (Princess Leia in *Star Wars*).

Wednesday 17: 22 die when Hurricane Alicia hits Texas.

The lyricist Ira Gershwin dies aged 86.

Thursday 18: Samantha Druce (GB), aged 12, becomes the youngest person to swim the English Channel to this date.

A major fire engulfs the historic Archbishop's Palace in the city of Trondheim, Norway.

Friday 19: Los Angeles councillor Gilbert Lindsay is slammed by critics for suggesting drunks and vagrants should be removed from the city's streets before the 1984 Olympics comes to town.

AUGUST 1983

Saturday 20: *Club Tropicana* by Wham! Peaks at number four in the UK singles charts.

Sunday 21: Benigno Aquino Jr, leader of the opposition in the Philippines, is assassinated.

Monday 22: Tabloid rumours of a new girlfriend for Prince Andrew, 23, are refuted when Buckingham Palace announces a 'mystery woman' spotted entering Balmoral Castle was regular guest Carolyn Herbert, daughter of the Queen's racing manager.

Tuesday 23: Actor Todd Bridges from the US TV comedy *Diff'rent Strokes* is arrested in Los Angeles on firearms offences.

A report by the Argentinian government recommends that the military junta which headed the invasion of the British Falkland Islands in 1982 be court-martialled.

Wednesday 24: Florence Thompson, 79, who was immortalised in Dorothea Lange's 1936 photograph of her as a victim of the Great Depression, is reported to be unable to pay her medical bills for a live-saving operation. Her family launches an appeal in the US media which raises $35,000.

Thursday 25: British Prime Minister Margaret Thatcher returns to work after a successful operation to repair a detached retina.

Friday 26: 44 people are killed when heavy rain causes flooding in Bilbao, Spain.

Saturday 27: Elton John's single *I'm Still Standing* peaks at number four in the UK charts.

On 24 August an appeal is launched for Florence Thompson, shown here in Dorothea Lange's iconic 1936 photograph 'Migrant Mother'.

AUGUST 1983

Rev Jesse Jackson: he leads commemorations in Washington on 27 August.

Civil rights campaigner Rev Jesse Jackson leads a march in Washington, DC, to commemorate the 20th anniversary of Martin Luther King's 'I have a dream' speech in 1963.

Sunday 28: Israel's Prime Minister Menachem Begin announces his resignation.

Monday 29: The ITV student quiz show *Blockbusters* hosted by Bob Holness is first broadcast.

Tuesday 30: The eighth NASA Space Shuttle mission begins.

Wednesday 31: Jean-Luc Godard's film *First Name: Carmen* wins the Lion d'Or at the Venice Film Festival.

Edwin Moses (USA) sets the world record for the 400m hurdles at 47.02 in Koblenz, Germany.

SEPTEMBER 1983

Thursday 1: 269 people including US Congressman Larry McDonald are killed when Soviet fighters shoot down Korean Airlines Flight 007 after it strayed into Soviet airspace.

Friday 2: The Soviet press agency Tass claims the incursion of the Korean airliner into Soviet airspace was deliberate in order to 'sow hostility'. The US Embassy in Moscow calls the statement 'preposterous'.

UB40 hits number one on 3 September.

Saturday 3: Commemorations take place in the USA to mark the bicentenary of the Treaty of Paris, the instrument which ended the Revolutionary War between the US and Britain.

Red Red Wine by UB40 hits number one in the UK singles charts.

Sunday 4: The Andrew Lloyd Webber musical *Joseph and His Amazing Technicolour Dreamcoat* closes on Broadway after 747 performances.

Monday 5: The eighth Space Shuttle mission ends.

SEPTEMBER 1983

**Yul Brynner in *The King and I.*
He completes his 400th performance on 13 September.**

Tuesday 6: Elmer Trett becomes the first motorcyclist to travel at over 200mph.

Wednesday 7: 1000 Americans of Korean origin clash with police in disturbances outside the Soviet mission in New York City following the shooting down of a Korean Airlines jet by Russian forces on 1 September.

Thursday 8: Britain's National Health Service privatises cleaning, catering and laundry services in a move estimated to save £90-180m per year.

Friday 9: The US tech giant Radio Shack (Tandy) launches its TRS-80 Colour Computer 2 PC.

Saturday 10: Larry Holmes defeats Scott Frank to win the World Heavyweight boxing title.

Martina Navratilova beats Chris Evert-Lloyd in the US Open women's tennis finals.

Sunday 11: Britain's Social Democratic Party votes against an alliance with the Liberal Party.

Jimmy Connors retains the US Open men's tennis title after defeating Ivan Lendl.

Vanessa Williams becomes Miss World on 17 September .

SEPTEMBER 1983

Monday 12: Albert Rizzo sets the world record for treading water at sea for 108 hours off the coast of Malta; he also becomes the first Maltese to enter the Guinness Book of Records.

Tuesday 13: Yul Brynner completes his 4000th performance in the musical *The King and I.*

After a lengthy probate enquiry, the estate of the late billionaire Howard Hughes, who died without making a will in 1976, is divided up between 22 distant relatives.

Wednesday 14: The singer Amy Winehouse is born in Enfield, London (died 2011).

Amy Winehouse is born on 14 September.

Thursday 15: Israel's Prime Minister Menachem Begin resigns.

An Indian 'Guru', Swami Vishnu Devananda, is briefly detained by East German police after flying a microlight aircraft over the Berlin Wall and distributing crysanthemums, to 'prove love and flowers can overcome barriers better than bombs.'

Friday 16: Actor Arnold Schwarzenegger becomes a US citizen.

Saturday 17: Vanessa Williams is crowned Miss America 1984, the first woman of African ancestry to win the title.

Sunday 18: The action series *Hardcastle and McCormick* is first shown on US TV.

Left: 'Arnie' becomes a US citizen on 16 September.

SEPTEMBER 1983

Britain's George Meegan becomes the first person to walk from the tip of South America to the north coast of Alaska. The feat took seven years and twelve pairs of boots.

Monday 19: Saint Kitts and Nevis is granted independence from Great Britain.

Tabloid speculation erupts over whether HRH Princess Diana is pregnant.

Tuesday 20: Soviet authorities announce they will return personal items found in the Korean airliner they shot down on 1 September, but no bodies will be repatriated.

Wednesday 21: David Mamet's play *Glengarry Glen Ross* opens in London.

Thursday 22: The redevelopment of London's Docklands begins with the opening of an Enterprise Zone on the Isle of Dogs.

Friday 23: 117 die when a bomb explodes on board Gulf Air Flight 771 over the United Arab Emirates.

Saturday 24: *Karma Chameleon* by Culture Club hits number one in the UK singles charts.

Lord Snowdon, ex-husband of HRH Princess Margaret, is temporarily blinded in a robbery attempt in West Kensington, London.

Sunday 25: 38 IRA prisoners escape from HM Prison Maze in Northern Ireland; one guard dies and 20 others are injured in the largest mass breakout in British history. The majority are eventually recaptured.

Karma Chameleon hits number one in the UK charts on 24 September.

SEPTEMBER 1983

Monday 26: A Soviet army officer, Lt Col Stanislav Petrov, averts a nuclear war by correctly identifying a warning of incoming US missiles as a false alarm.

Tuesday 27: The first major free open-source software, the GNU Project, is announced in the USA by programmer Richard Stallman.

Police arrest a man who attempts to attack British Prime Minister Margaret Thatcher while she enters a Toronto hotel on a speaking tour.

Wednesday 28: Soviet premier Yuri Andropov rejects arms limitation proposals by US President Ronald Reagan.

Lilian Gish receives a Lifetime Achievement Award on 30 September.

Thursday 29: The 3389th performance of *A Chorus Line* makes it the longest running Broadway show to this date.

Dame Mary Donaldson becomes the first woman Lord Mayor of London.

Friday 30: The International Federation of Airline Pilots' Association calls for an end to the boycott of Russian airports imposed since the shooting down of a Korean airliner on 1 September.

Silent film star Lilian Gish is given a Lifetime Achievement Award by the American Film Institute.

Bill Morgan, 36, becomes the first blind man to walk from coast to coast across the USA.

OCTOBER 1983

Saturday 1: *Total Eclipse of the Heart* by Bonnie Tyler hits number one in the US singles charts.

Sunday 2: Neil Kinnock becomes leader of the Labour Party.

Monday 3: Michael Jackson and Paul McCartney's single *Say Say Say* is released.

Tuesday 4: Richard Noble (GB) sets a new land speed record of 633 mph (1019 kph) driving *Thrust 2* in the Nevada desert.

Wednesday 5: The Polish Solidarity leader Lech Walesa is awarded the Nobel Peace Prize.

Neil Kinnock becomes leader of HM Loyal Opposition on 2 October.

Thursday 6: Author William Golding (*Lord of the Flies*) is awarded the Nobel Prize for Literature.

Friday 7: Plans to dissolve the Greater London Council are announced; despite protests the body is closed down in 1986 and later replaced with the Greater London Assembly.

44 civilian hostages are exchanged by rival factions in the conflict in Beirut, Lebanon.

OCTOBER 1983

Saturday 8: US President Reagan's commission on Central America begins, with a six day, six nation tour of the region by US officials.

Sunday 9: A failed assassination attempt, most probably by North Koreans, is made on Chun Doo-Whan, president of South Korea. The bombing, which takes place during a state visit to Burma, kills 21 people including foreign minister Lee Beom-Seok.

Monday 10: Yitzhak Shamir becomes Prime Minister of Israel.

Tuesday 11: Bryant Pond, Maine, becomes the last US town to change from a hand-cranked telephone service with local switchboard to a modern direct-dial system.

Wednesday 12: Kakuei Tanaka, former Prime Minister of Japan, is sentenced to four years in prison after being convicted of taking $2m in bribes from aircraft manufacturer Lockheed.

The first commercial mobile phone, the Motorola DynaTAC 8000X, goes into use on 13 October.

Thursday 13: The world's first commercial mobile phone service goes into operation, as Ameritech president Bob Barnett makes a call from Chicago to Germany to speak to the great-grandson of Alexander Graham-Bell, inventor of the first telephone in 1876.

Friday 14: Britain's Trade and Industry Secretary Cecil Parkinson resigns over allegations of an affair with his secretary, Sara Keays.

Saturday 15: Actor Pat O'Brien (*Angels with Dirty Faces*) dies aged 83.

Sunday 16: Tom Watson wins the US Ryder Cup golf tournament.

Left: Pat O'Brien dies on 15 October.

OCTOBER 1983

Maurice Bishop, Prime Minister of Grenada, is deposed in a military coup.

Monday 17: US astronomer Carl Sagan announces the launch of META (Megachannel Extraterrestrial Assay) at Harvard University; a computer system able to scan millions of radio frequencies in the hope of finding signals from intelligent aliens.

Tuesday 18: Pope John Paul II holds talks with Sweden's Prime Minister Olaf Palme in the Vatican, following a resumption of diplomatic relations between the two states after a 455-year lapse.

Wednesday 19: Maurice Bishop, the recently deposed Prime Minister of Grenada, is assassinated.

The two Metropolitan Police officers who shot Stephen Waldorf in London on 14 January are cleared of attempted murder.

The US Senate approves the setting up of a national holiday to commemorate the civil rights campaigner Martin Luther King.

Thursday 20: The US National Academy of Sciences warns in a report that civilization has just twenty years to deal with global warming and climate change.

Friday 21: The General Conference on Weights and Measures redefines the international definition of a metre as the distance light travels in a vacuum in 1/299,792/458th of a second.

Men of the Royal Barbados Police arrive in Grenada on 25 October as part of a joint US/Commonwealth invasion force.

OCTOBER 1983

Saturday 22: Up to one million people are estimated to attend a march against nuclear weapons in London organised by CND (The Campaign for Nuclear Disarmament).

A drunken intruder, Charles Harris, holds five aides hostage at the Augusta Golf Club and demands to speak to President Reagan who is staying at the resort. He is arrested after letting the hostages go to fetch him some whisky.

Sunday 23: 241 US and 58 French servicemen are killed along with six civilians in two attacks by Islamic militants in Beirut, Lebanon.

Sir Paul Scoon, Governor of Grenada, appeals for calm on 29 October.

Monday 24: The serial killer Dennis Nilsen goes on trial at the Old Bailey, London.

Tuesday 25: US troops invade Grenada in response to the recent violent coup and assassination of its Prime Minister, Maurice Bishop.

Multi-Tool Word, the prototype of Microsoft Word software, is release in the USA.

The US vessel *Glomar Java Sea* goes missing during a typhoon in the South China Seas, all 82 hands are presumed dead.

Wednesday 26: Widespread condemnation of the US invasion of Grenada appears in the media particularly from the UK, since the island is part of the British Commonwealth.

Thursday 27: US President Ronald Reagan defends the invasion of Grenada, stating his forces got there 'just in time' to prevent a takeover by Cuban communists.

Friday 28: Israeli archaeologist Adam Zartal announces his discovery of a 3000 year old altar on Mount Ebal thought to be that mentioned in the Biblical book of Joshua.

OCTOBER 1983

Saturday 29: Sir Paul Scoon, Governor-General of Grenada, calls for government employees to return to work as US troops announce the capture of coup leader Bernard Coard.

Sunday 30: US investigators into the Beirut bombings of 23 October which killed over 300 people conclude they were carried out using food delivery lorries which had not been checked by sentries.

Monday 31: It is announced that the address book of Marilyn Monroe, who died in 1962, is to be auctioned; it includes the details of several well known Hollywood stars.

NOVEMBER 1983

Tuesday 1: The wreck of the *Glomar Java Sea*, which went missing on 25 October, is located by sonar on the bed of the South China Sea at a depth of 300 feet.

Wednesday 2: The government of South Africa grants limited political rights to asians and coloureds (people of mixed race).

The Michael Jackson single *Thriller* is released.

Thriller is released on 2 November.

Thursday 3: Rival factions of the Palestinian Liberation Organisation (PLO) clash in the Battle of Tripoli.

Friday 4: The serial killer Dennis Nilsen, of Muswell Hill, London N10, is sentenced to life imprisonment.

Saturday 5: Five workers are killed in an explosion on the Byford Dolphin oil rig in the North Sea.

NOVEMBER 1983

Marvin Hagler retains his World Heavyweight title on 10 November.

Uptown Girl by Billy Joel hits number one in the UK singles chart.

Sunday 6: The hairdresser Vidal Sassoon marries dressage champion Jeanette Hartford Davis.

The bodies of 100 people, presumed to include that of recently assassinated Prime Minister Maurice Bishop, are discovered by occupying US forces in a remote part of Grenada.

Monday 7: The last nuclear scare of the Cold War takes place when Soviet officials misinterpret the NATO exercise 'Able Archer' as an actual attack. The incident is later dramatised in the TV series *Deutschland '83*.

A bomb placed by communists explodes in the US Senate; nobody is injured.

Tuesday 8: Battle of Tripoli: PLO leader Yasser Arafat calls for a truce with the rival factions with whom he has been in combat since 3 November.

Wednesday 9: Sir Paul Scoon, Governor-General of Grenada, appoints a nine-member provisional government following the recent coup attempt which was put down by invading US forces.

Yasser Arafat calls for peace on 8 November.

Brewing magnate Freddy Heineken is kidnapped in Amsterdam. He is released on 30 November after a ransom payment of 35 million Guilders (about £15.7m)

Thursday 10: Marvin Hagler retains his World Middleweight boxing title in a bout with Roberto Duran in Las Vegas.

Friday 11: US President Ronald Reagan becomes the first western leader to address Japan's Parliament.

NOVEMBER 1983

Saturday 12: Pope John Paul II gives a speech urging Catholics not to work in weapons research.

Sunday 13: The first US Cruise missiles arrive at RAF Greenham Common in Berkshire; a permanent protest camp is set up nearby.

Monday 14: HM Queen Elizabeth II begins a four day state visit to Bangladesh.

Tuesday 15: The Turkish Republic of Northern Cyprus declares itself independent.

300 people are arrested during anti-Cruise missile protests outside London's Houses of Parliament.

Gerry Adams becomes leader of Irish nationalist party Sinn Fein.

US President Ronald Reagan and his wife Nancy with Emperor Hirohito at the start of the US state visit on 9 November.

Wednesday 16: 20 English football hooligans are arrested following violent disorder in Luxembourg after England fails to qualify for the 1984 European Cup.

Debra Winger stars in *Terms of Endearment*, released on 20 November.

Thursday 17: The film *Yentl*, starring Barbra Streisand, premieres.

Friday 18: The world's first surviving set of all-female sextuplets is born in Liverpool, to Janet and Graham Walton.

NOVEMBER 1983

Terry Pratchett's first *Discworld* novel is published on 24 November.

Saturday 19: 8 Georgian nationalists are killed by security forces in a failed hijacking attempt of an airliner in Georgia, USSR.

Sunday 20: The oscar-winning film *Terms of Endearment* starring Shirley Maclaine and Debra Winger premieres in New York City.

The nuclear war film *The Day After* is watched by c.100 million people, the highest ever ratings for a TV movie, when broadcast in the USA.

Three people are killed and seven wounded when IRA gunmen open fire in a Protestant church in Darkly, County Armagh.

Monday 21: HM Queen Elizabeth II addresses the military academy at Poona as part of her Indian tour.

Tuesday 22: Actor Michael Conrad, star of TV's *Hill Street Blues* series and famous for his character's catchphrase 'Let's be careful out there!' dies aged 58.

Wednesday 23: Britain's M54 motorway opens.

Thursday 24: Fantasy author Terry Pratchett's first *Discworld* novel, *The Colour of Magic*, is published.

Friday 25: Larry Holmes knocks out Marvis Frazier in the first round to win the World Heavyweight boxing championship in Las Vegas.

Michael Conrad dies on 22 November.

NOVEMBER 1983

Saturday 26: Gold bars worth nearly £26m are stolen from a Brinks-Mat security vault at Heathrow Airport, London. Although two men are later convicted, only a fraction of the gold is ever recovered.

Sunday 27: 181 people are killed when Colombian Avianca Flight 11 crashes near Madrid, Spain.

Monday 28: NASA's Space Shuttle Columbia begins its sixth mission. Astronaut Ulf Merbold becomes the first non-American to fly in the Shuttle and the first West German in space.

Ulf Merbold becomes the first West German in space on 28 November.

Tuesday 29: Scotland Yard detectives investigating the Brinks-Mat robbery of 26 November announce a £2m reward for information leading to a conviction.

Wednesday 30: Radio Shack launches the Tandy 2000 personal computer.

The kidnapped Dutch beer magnate Freddie Heineken is released unharmed after payment of a £15.7m ransom.

Left: The Tandy 2000 PC is launched on 30 November.

DECEMBER 1983

Thursday 1: The Roman Catholic church publishes *Educational Guidance in Human Love*, a traditionally-minded approach to marriage and sexual matters, disappointing some who had hoped for a more liberal stance by the Vatican.

Friday 2: Blizzards bring record snowfalls to the USA's Rocky Mountains, with falls of up to 12' recorded in some places.

Saturday 3: USAF jet fighters shoot down two Lebanese aircraft in the first aerial confrontation of the US peacekeeping mission.

Sunday 4: An annular solar eclipse takes place, visible from most of Africa.

Two IRA gunmen are shot dead in a confrontation with British soldiers on a routine patrol in County Tyrone.

Eight US marines are killed in clashes with insurgents in the Lebanon.

Monday 5: The first successful heart and lung transplant in Britain is carried out at London's Harefield Hospital.

Tuesday 6: The record for the highest price paid for art is set at $11.7m when 12th century book *The Gospels of Henry de Lion* is auctioned to a West German consortium at Sotheby's, London.

DECEMBER 1983

An illustration from *The Gospels of Henry de Lion,* sold for $11.7m on 6 December.

Wednesday 7: 90 people are killed when two planes collide in fog at Madrid airport, Spain.

Thursday 8: Britain's House of Lords votes to allow televised coverage of its proceedings.

Friday 9: The Australian dollar is floated for the first time, after being fixed against the US dollar and before that, the pound sterling.

Saturday 10: Raul Alfonsin becomes President of Argentina, returning the country to civilian rule.

Only You by the Flying Pickets hits number one in the UK singles charts.

Sunday 11: Pope John Paul II makes the first papal visit to a Lutheran church, in Rome.

Mats Wilander beats Ivan Lendl to win the Australian Open men's tennis tournament.

DECEMBER 1983

Monday 12: Five people are killed in a truck bomb attack on the US Embassy in Kuwait.

Tuesday 13: A civilian government takes over in Turkey under Turgut Ozal.

Wednesday 14: The USS *New Jersey* shells Syrian positions in Lebanon for the first time, as President Reagan announces the USA is not there to 'enter into combat'.

Thursday 15: An 'unofficial' James Bond film, *Never Say Never Again* starring Sean Connery in the title role, is released. The film begins the infamous 'Battle of the Bonds' as it competes with the 'official' film *Octopussy*.

Friday 16: Pete Townshend, lead singer of The Who, announces the band is breaking up.

Saturday 17: 83 people are killed in a fire at the Alcala nightclub in Madrid, Spain.

6 people are killed and 90 injured when an IRA car-bomb explodes outside Harrod's department store in London.

Sunday 18: The Rolling Stones guitarist Keith Richards marries model Patti Hansen.

Monday 19: For the second time in its history the Jules Rimet World Cup trophy is stolen when the Brazilian

Left: US First Lady Nancy Reagan sits on the lap of 'Santa' (*A-Team* star 'Mr T') to publicise the 'Just Say No' anti-drugs campaign on 12 December.

DECEMBER 1983

Bob Hope entertains US troops in the Lebanon on 23 December. Stars include Miss USA Julie Hayek (far left) and actress Brooke Shields (far right).

Soccer Confederation in Rio is raided. Unlike the 1966 theft the trophy is never recovered, and a replacement is made in 1984.

Tuesday 20: Yassar Arafat, leader of the Palestinian Liberation Organisation, evacuates his 4000 followers from the Lebanon.

Wednesday 21: Four suspects in the Harrods bombing case of 17 December are arrested in London after a series of police raids.

Thursday 22: PLO leader Yasser Arafat meets for talks with Egypt's President Hosni Mubarak.

Friday 23: Bob Hope entertains US troops in the Lebanon with a show on board the USS *New Jersey*.

Saturday 24: Actor Johnny Depp marries make-up artist Lori Anne Alison.

Sunday 25: Christmas celebrations in Bethlehem are swelled for the first time by thousands of US servicemen on leave from nearby Lebanon. 150 'peace pilgrims' arrive in the town after having taken 18 months to walk there from Seattle, Washington in an anti-nuclear protest.

DECEMBER 1983

US President Ronald Reagan and Soviet premier Yuri Andropov are voted *Time* magazine's Men of the Year on 26 December.

20 fireman are called to the Tower of London for a blaze caused by a Christmas pudding catching fire in an oven.

A second IRA bomb explodes outside Harrod's department store in London; nobody is injured as the shop is closed.

The Spanish painter and sculptor Joan Miró dies aged 90.

Monday 26: Comedian Bob Hope entertains US servicemen in Beirut.

US President Ronald Reagan and Soviet premier Yuri Andropov are announced as *Time* Magazine's Men of the Year.

Tuesday 27: Pope John Paul II visits his would-be assassin, Mehmet Ali Agca in prison to offer his forgiveness.

Wednesday 28: Dennis Wilson, 39, drummer with The Beach Boys, drowns while swimming off the California coast.

Thursday 29: India's Sunil Gavaskar makes cricketing history when he scores his 30th century and fourth test double-century in the sixth test against the West Indies in Madras.

The USA announces its withdrawal from UNESCO (United Nations Educational, Scientific and Cultural Organisation) over its perceived anti-western bias.

Friday 30: Europe's first Pershing 2 missiles are installed at the US Army base at Mutlangen, West Germany. 20 anti-nuclear protestors are arrested after attempting to block the main gate.

Saturday 31: The British colony of Brunei becomes independent at midnight.

President Shehu Shaghari of Nigeria is ousted in a military coup.

Other titles from Montpelier Publishing:

A Little Book of Limericks:
Funny Rhymes for all the Family
ISBN 9781511524124

Scottish Jokes: A Wee Book of Clean Caledonian Chuckles
ISBN 9781495297366

The Old Fashioned Joke Book:
Gags and Funny Stories
ISBN 9781514261989

Non-Religious Funeral Readings:
Philosophy and Poetry for Secular Services
ISBN 9781500512835

Large Print Jokes: Hundreds of Gags in Easy-to-Read Type
ISBN 9781517775780

Spiritual Readings for Funerals and Memorial Services
ISBN 9781503379329

Victorian Murder: True Crimes, Confessions and Executions
ISBN 9781530296194

Large Print Prayers: A Prayer for Each Day of the Month
ISBN 9781523251476

A Little Book of Ripping Riddles and Confounding Conundrums
ISBN 9781505548136

Vinegar uses: over 150 ways to use vinegar
ISBN 9781512136623

Large Print Wordsearch:
100 Puzzles in Easy-to-Read Type
ISBN 9781517638894

The Pipe Smoker's Companion
ISBN 9781500441401

The Book of Church Jokes
ISBN 9781507620632

Bar Mitzvah Notebook
ISBN 9781976007781

Jewish Jokes
ISBN 9781514845769

Large Print Address Book
ISBN 9781539820031

How to Cook Without a Kitchen:
Easy, Healthy and Low-Cost Meals
9781515340188

Large Print Birthday Book
ISBN 9781544670720

Retirement Jokes
ISBN 9781519206350

Take my Wife: Hilarious Jokes of Love and Marriage
ISBN 9781511790956

Welsh Jokes: A Little Book of Wonderful Welsh Wit
ISBN 9781511612241

1001 Ways to Save Money: Thrifty Tips for the Fabulously Frugal!
ISBN 9781505432534

Available online at Amazon

Printed in Great Britain
by Amazon

27288208R00036